If She Can Do It, I Can, Too!

By

De'Shawna Yamini

Illustrated by Ayzha Middlebrooks

Published by
Queen V Publishing
Englewood, OH
QueenVPublishing.com

Published by Queen V Publishing
Englewood, OH
QueenVPublishing.com

Copyright © 2021 by De'Shawna Yamini

All rights reserved. The author guarantees all writings are original works and do not infringe upon the legal rights of any other person living or deceased. No part of this book can be reproduced in any form without written permission from the author.

Library of Congress Control Number: 2021922187

ISBN-13: 978-0-9962991-8-3

Cover design and illustrations by Ayzha Middlebrooks

Edited by Valerie J. Lewis Coleman of Pen of the Writer PenOfTheWriter.com

Proofread by Ethleen Sawyerr of Speak, Write, Play

Photo credit: Kendra DeCaille

Printed in the United States of America

This book is for you,
young and old,
to be inspired
by the strong and bold.
To understand how great you will be,
let's learn from Black HERstory!

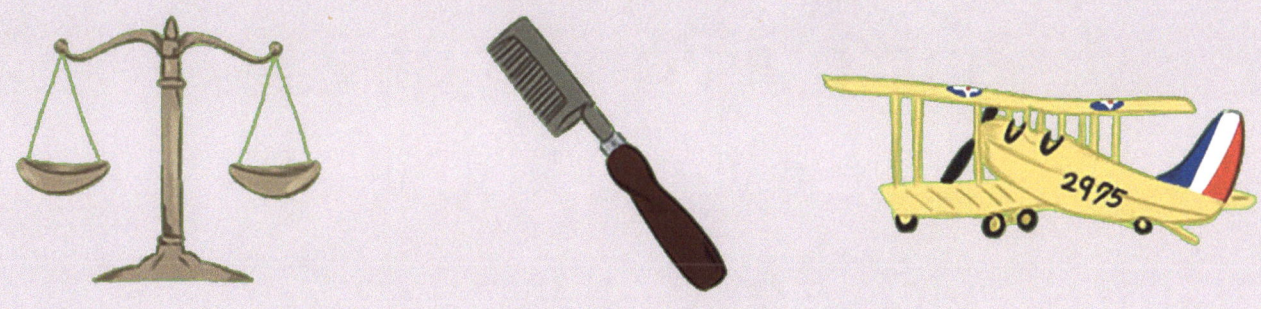

A note from Mrs. DY: The illustrations of Mary McLeod Bethune, Dr. Mamie Phipps Clark, and Augusta Savage have skin tones in grayscale. Due to the lack of color photos of these women, we did not want to misrepresent them.

Young Miss Sarah
was losing her hair
but soon became a millionaire.
She created products
to make hair grow,
and built an empire
so now you know!
Madam C.J. Walker
made her dream come true.
If she can do it,
I can, too.

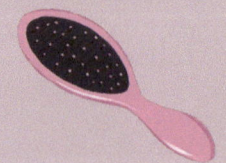

Madam C.J. Walker
(born Sarah Breedlove)
(1867 - 1919)

Madam C.J. Walker was an entrepreneur and social activist who created a haircare empire, becoming the first self-made woman millionaire! Madam Walker said that the ingredients for her hair formula came to her in a dream.

Mary was part
of a large family.
The first to go to school
was the way it had to be!
She shared what she learned
with everyone in the house.
And as an adult, she started
a college in the South!
Bethune Cookman
is the college she grew.
If she can educate,
I can, too!

Mary McLeod Bethune
(1875 - 1955)

Mary McLeod Bethune started a private school, which became Bethune Cookman College, a historically Black College or University (HBCU). She was the founder of the National Council for Negro Women. She also served as an advisor for President Franklin D. Roosevelt. The role made her the highest-ranking Black woman in government at the time.

Bessie Coleman
was determined to fly
an airplane as high
as it could go in the sky!
In America, she wasn't
allowed to learn.
So she went to France
and worked to earn
a pilot's license
and away she flew!
If she learned to fly,
I can, too!

Bessie Coleman
(1892 - 1926)

Bessie Coleman was the first Black woman and first Native American to earn a pilot's license. Forbidden to attend flight school in the United States because she was a woman of color, Bessie earned her pilot's license from the Fédération Aéronautique Internationale in France in 1921.

Augusta was a leading talent
in her day,
an amazing sculptor
and master of clay.
She crafted beautiful things,
large and small,
and gigantic creations
sixteen feet tall!
Augusta's praise is long overdue.
If she could create,
I can, too!

Augusta Savage
(1892 - 1962)

Augusta Savage was a sculptor during the famed Harlem Renaissance. As a child, she used the natural red clay around her home to sculpt. Her most notable work was *Lift Every Voice and Sing,* inspired by the song also known as "The Black National Anthem."

Ella Jo Baker
was a powerful force.
She worked behind the scenes
and stayed the course.
She organized youth
to fight for change
through many different groups
that she arranged!
For over fifty years,
it was HER, it's true.
If she made it happen,
I can, too!

Ella Jo Baker
(1903 - 1986)

Ella Jo Baker, a graduate of Shaw University, was a civil rights activist and organizer. She served as a leader within organizations such as the Southern Christian Leadership Conference (SCLC), the National Association for the Advancement of Colored People (NAACP), and a leader within the Student Nonviolent Coordinating Committee (SNCC).

Dr. Mamie Clark
studied the human mind.
Alongside her husband,
the two would find
that little Black children
had low self-esteem.
They made sure
children followed their dreams
by helping to end
segregation in schools.
If she changed their minds,
I can, too!

Dr. Mamie Phipps Clark
(1917 - 1983)

Dr. Clark and her husband, Kenneth, were the first Black Americans to earn doctoral degrees in psychology from Columbia University. Dr. Clark was the psychologist who developed the famous doll study that proved segregation caused psychological harm to Black children. Her study played a pivotal role in the 1954 Brown v. Board of Education case.

Fannie Lou Hamer
made a choice
to encourage Black people
to use their voice.
By voting in elections
when they didn't have the right,
Fannie Lou was ready to fight.
She fought for voting rights
for me and for you.
If she fought for freedom,
I can, too!

Fannie Lou Hamer
(1917 - 1977)

Fannie Lou Hamer was a civil rights activist for American voting and women's rights. She was the co-founder of the Mississippi Freedom Democratic Party, as well as one of the organizers of Freedom Summer, an event that helped increase Black voter registration in the South.

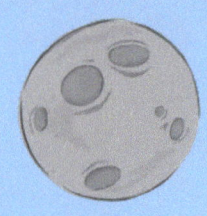

Katherine Johnson created a path
from Earth to space by using math.
She solved the problems
that would soon
send astronauts to the moon.
She did the work
a computer could do.
If she can do it,
I can, too!

Katherine Johnson
(1918 - 2020)

Mrs. Johnson was a gifted student, graduating high school at age fourteen. She attended West Virginia State College, where she graduated four years later with degrees in French and mathematics. She worked for NASA, calculating astronauts' flight trajectories during the early days of space travel.

 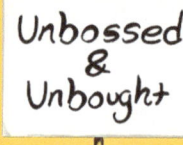

Shirley Chisholm
paved the way
for women of color
to run today.
For public office
she paid the cost,
and ran her life
"Unbought and Unbossed."
Shirley was a leader
who saw it through.
If she can lead,
I can, too!

Shirley Chisholm
(1924 - 2005)

In 1968, Shirley Chisolm became the first Black woman elected to the U.S. Congress. From 1969 to 1983, she represented the Twelfth Congressional District of New York. In 1972, she became the first Black woman to run for president of the United States. Her campaign slogan was "Unbought and Unbossed."

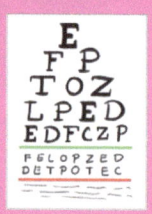

Patricia Bath was the best in school!
Earned her diploma in two years,
that's way too cool!
She went to Howard
for a medical degree
and was the first Black woman
in oph-thal-mol-o-gy!
She was a doctor and inventor
who deserves her due.
If she did it,
I can, too!

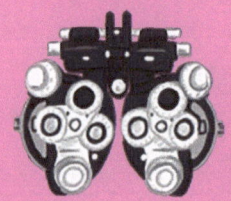

Dr. Patricia Bath
(1942 - 2019)

Dr. Bath was the first Black woman to complete a residency in ophthalmology, the area of medicine and surgery that deals with disorders of the eyes. Dr. Bath is also the inventor of the Laserphaco Probe, a device used in cataract surgery.

Dr. Mae Jemison did it all,
an engineer and physician
before answering the call.
To become an astronaut
and go to outer space,
her many achievements
will never be erased.
Dr. Mae is amazing.
What else can she do?
If she can do it,
I can, too!

Dr. Mae Jemison
(1956 -)

Astronaut, engineer, and physician, Dr. Jemison entered Stanford University at age sixteen, earning degrees in chemical engineering and African American studies. She earned a medical degree from Cornell Medical School.

For two hundred thirty-two years,
the VP looked the same.
Then along came a woman
who changed the game!
She might be the first,
but she won't be the last.
History has been made;
the glass ceiling is smashed!
Brown-skinned girl,
your VP looks like you.
If she can do it,
I can, too!

Kamala Harris
(1964 -)

Kamala Harris, the 49th vice president of the United States, is the first woman and first person of African and Asian descent to be elected to the office. Before being elected as vice president, she served in the U.S. Senate and was the attorney general of California.

These women are proof,
it is easy to see,
that nothing limits
what you can do or be!

Whatever you choose
to do with your days,

be encouraged and excited
as you determine the ways!

Work hard and learn much
as you figure things out.
You will find yourself
as you travel your route!

You are smart and talented
like those who came before.
You've seen what they did,
and you can do more!

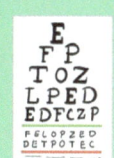

Some had setbacks
before they won.
Just believe and keep going
until your work is done!

You can have anything you want
when your heart believes it's true.
If they can do it,
YOU CAN, TOO!

Learn more about these amazing women by visiting the following websites:

Ella Jo Baker	EllaBakerCenter.org/who-was-ella-baker
Dr. Patricia Bath	CFMedicine.nlm.nih.gov/physicians/biography_26.html
Mary McLeod Bethune	WomensHistory.org/education-resources/biographies/mary-mcleod-bethune
Shirley Chisholm	History.House.gov/People/Listing/C/CHISHOLM,-Shirley-Anita-(C000371)/
Dr. Mamie Phipps Clark	APA.org/pi/oema/resources/ethnicity-health/psychologists/clark
Bessie Coleman	WomensHistory.org/education-resources/biographies/bessie-coleman
Fannie Lou Hamer	WomensHistory.org/education-resources/biographies/fannie-lou-hamer
Kamala Harris	WhiteHouse.gov/administration/vice-president-harris
Dr. Mae Jemison	WomensHistory.org/education-resources/biographies/mae-jemison
Katherine Johnson	NASA.gov/content/katherine-johnson-biography
Augusta Savage	AmericanArt.si.edu/artist/augusta-savage-4269
Madam C.J. Walker	MadamCJWalker.com

If She Can Do It, I Can, Too Trivia Questions

After you've read more about the women featured in this book, answer the following questions:

1. Two sets of women were born in the same year. Who are they?
2. Which woman lived to be over 100 years old?
3. Name the women who are members of Alpha Kappa Alpha Sorority, Inc.
4. Name the women who are members of Delta Sigma Theta Sorority, Inc.
5. Who founded the National Council for Negro Women?
6. Name the women who attended Howard University.
7. Who received an education or lessons outside of the United States?
8. Name the three women who graduated early from high school.
9. Who had over ten siblings?
10. Name the woman who was born on Leap Day (February 29).
11. How many women earned the right to be called "doctor" by obtaining doctoral degrees?
12. Which women speak more than one language?

Answers: 1. Fannie Lou Hamer and Dr. Mamie Phipps Clark (1917); Bessie Coleman and Augusta Savage (1892) 2. Katherine Johnson (101) 3. Dr. Patricia Bath, Dr. Mae Jemison (honorary), Katherine Johnson, Kamala Harris 4. Fannie Lou Hamer (honorary), Elle Jo Baker, Shirley Chisholm, Mary McLeod Bethune 5. Mary McLeod Bethune 6. Dr. Patricia Bath, Kamala Harris, Dr. Mamie Phipps Clark 7. Bessie Coleman (France), Shirley Chisholm (Barbados), Augusta Savage (France) 8. Katherine Johnson, Dr. Mae Jemison, Dr. Patricia Bath 9. Fannie Lou Hamer (19), Mary McLeod Bethune (16), Augusta Savage (13), Bessie Coleman (12) 10. Augusta Savage 11. Dr. Patricia Bath, Dr. Mamie Phipps Clark, Dr. Mae Jemison 12. Bessie Coleman (French), Dr. Mae Jemison (Russian, Japanese, Swahili), Katherine Johnson (French), Shirley Chisholm (Spanish)

Mrs. DY wants to hear about the women who inspire you. Whether mentioned in *If She Can Do It, I Can, Too,* someone you admire from afar, or women you personally know, send an email to MrsDY@IfSheCanDoIt.me describing how they influence you to reach your dreams.